THE STORY OF THE GOSPEL

HALEY WARNER

WestBow Press books may be ordered through booksellers or by contacting:

WestBow Press
A Division of Thomas Nelson & Zondervan
1663 Liberty Drive
Bloomington, IN 47403
www.westbowpress.com
844-714-3454

Scripture taken from the King James Version of the Bible.

ISBN: 978-1-6642-2646-3 (sc)
ISBN: 978-1-6642-2648-7 (hc)
ISBN: 978-1-6642-2647-0 (e)

Library of Congress Control Number: 2021904505

Print information available on the last page.

WestBow Press rev. date: 06/14/2021

WestBow
P R E S S®
A DIVISION OF THOMAS NELSON
& ZONDERVAN

A NOTE TO PARENTS

This book tells the story of God's amazing grace and His plan of salvation in simple terms.

While we sometimes assume that salvation is an adult decision that kids should not be expected to make, Jesus Himself knew that God's truths are revealed even to young children when He prayed, "I thank thee, O Father, Lord of heaven and earth, because thou hast hid these things from the wise and prudent, and hast revealed them unto babes." (Matt 11:25)

While salvation is a one-time event, sharing the gospel and helping your children grow in their faith should happen all the time. I encourage you to reflect on God's word often with your children and I hope this book can help facilitate those conversations in your home.

And that from a child thou hast known the holy scriptures, which are able to make thee wise unto salvation through faith which is in Christ Jesus.

2 Timothy 3:15

God is perfect
and He created
everything.

Genesis 1:1 In the beginning God created the heaven and the earth.

He made the sun to shine, stars to twinkle, grass to grow.

He made fish to swim,
bugs to crawl, birds
to fly and, finally, He
made two people:
Adam and Eve.

Genesis 1:27 So God created man in his own image, in the image
of God created he him; male and female created he them.

God made rules to protect His creation, perfect rules that divide right from wrong.

Rev 4:11 Thou art worthy, O Lord, to receive glory and honour and power: for thou hast created all things, and for thy pleasure they are and were created.

Everything was made to show God's goodness and everything was perfect.

But then something happened.

An evil serpent tricked Adam and Eve, and they broke God's rules.

God's perfect creation wasn't perfect anymore.

You might not think it's
a big deal, but when
you break God's rules,
the Bible calls it sin.

Sin is always a
big deal to God.

Romans 5:12 Wherefore, as by one man sin entered into the world, and death by sin; and so death passed upon all men, for that all have sinned.

Because Adam and Eve first sinned, all people will always sin.

Romans 3:23 For all have sinned and fall short of the glory of God

Sometimes we use a bad word or we're mean to our brother.

Sometimes we tell a lie or we want what our friend has.

There's no one on Earth
that doesn't sin.

Romans 3:10 As it is written, there is none righteous, no, not one.

Sin keeps us away from God.
Because God is perfectly fair,
sin must be punished.

Isaiah 59:2 But your iniquities have separated between you and your
God, and your sins have hid his face from you, that he will not hear.

The punishment for sin is death and separation from God in a place called Hell.

Romans 6:23 For the wages of sin is death, but the gift of God is eternal life in Christ Jesus our Lord.

But God loves us and has a plan to rescue us from our sin, so we can live with Him and enjoy His goodness forever.

It's called salvation.

Romans 5:8 But God commendeth his love toward us, in that, while we were yet sinners, Christ died for us.

This is God's plan of salvation:
He came to Earth himself,
as a baby named Jesus!

**Jesus lived a perfect
life and never sinned,
not even once.**

John 1:14 And the Word became flesh and dwelt among
us, and we have seen his glory, glory as of the only Son
from the Father, full of grace and truth.

Jesus never had a bad thought.

Or took something that didn't belong to Him.

Hebrews 7:26 For such an high priest became us, who is holy, harmless, undefiled, separate from sinners, and made higher than the heavens.

He never loved
anything more
than God.

Or forgot to say,
"I'm sorry."

Even though He was perfect,
Jesus was beaten and put
to death on a cross.

But this, too,
was part of
God's plan.

Jesus allowed himself to be punished instead of us. He died in our place.

1 Peter 2:24 Who his own self bare our sins in his own body on the tree, that we, being dead to sins, should live unto righteousness: by whose stripes ye were healed.

**Three days later,
He came back to life.
This is the gospel:
the good news!**

2 Cor 5:17 Therefore if any man be in Christ, he is a new creature: old things are passed away; behold, all things are become new.

Jesus died for us so we can be
forgiven for our sins and be a
part of God's family forever.

Salvation is a free gift offered to the entire world.

But just like any gift,
you have to accept it
before it's yours.

Ephesians 2:8 For by grace are ye saved through faith; and that not of yourselves: it is the gift of God.

God wants you and all people to accept His gift of salvation, but it's your choice.

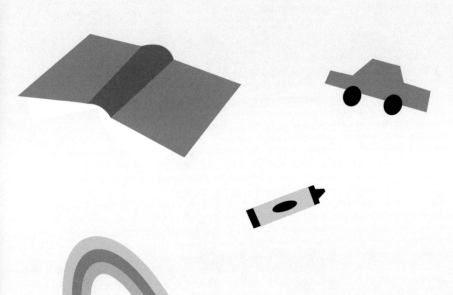

When you believe that Jesus is God and that He died so you can be forgiven of your sins, you receive God's gift of salvation.

Romans 10:9 That if thou shalt confess with thy mouth the Lord Jesus, and shalt believe in thine heart that God hath raised him from the dead, thou shalt be saved

In that very moment,
you are saved.

Jesus is coming back
soon, and all creation will
be made perfect again

just like it was in
the beginning.

God's children will
live with Him in
Heaven forever.

And never be separated from Him again.

John 10:28 And I give unto them eternal life; and they shall never perish, neither shall any man pluck them out of my hand.

Printed in the United States
by Baker & Taylor Publisher Services